IMPRESSIONS FOR PIANO

20 PIECES

FOR STUDENTS

BY

André Previn

ISBN 978-0-7935-6148-3

HAL•LEONARD®
CORPORATION

7777 W. BLUEMOUND RD. P.O. BOX 13819 MILWAUKEE, WI 53213

Visit Hal Leonard Online at
www.halleonard.com

To Claudia and Alicia

1. GOOD MORNING

ANDRE PREVIN

MCA music publishing

2. POLAR BEAR DANCE

ANDRÉ PREVIN

3. PROMENADE IN THE PARK

ANDRÉ PREVIN

4. POODLES

ANDRÉ PREVIN

5. BY A QUIET STREAM

ANDRÉ PREVIN

6. PARADE OF THE PENGUINS

ANDRÉ PREVIN

7. TREES AT TWILIGHT

ANDRÉ PREVIN

Simply ♩ = 66

8. MECHANICAL TOY

ANDRÉ PREVIN

9. PROCESSION WITH LANTERNS

ANDRÉ PREVIN

10. IN PERPETUAL MOTION

ANDRÉ PREVIN

11. ROUNDUP

ANDRÉ PREVIN

12. A PIECE OF LACE

ANDRÉ PREVIN

13. THE OUT- OF- TUNE BAND

ANDRÉ PREVIN

Gaily ♩=112

14. DESERT FLOWERS

ANDRÉ PREVIN

15. MINIATURE MARCH

ANDRÉ PREVIN

16. A GENTLE THOUGHT

ANDRÉ PREVIN

17. MIMICRY

ANDRÉ PREVIN

Gaily ♩=132

18. SWANS

ANDRÉ PREVIN

19. CAREFREE MOOD

ANDRÉ PREVIN

20. SCHERZO

ANDRÉ PREVIN